Anonymous

Georgia before the Senate Judiciary Committee

Anonymous

Georgia before the Senate Judiciary Committee

ISBN/EAN: 9783337161507

Printed in Europe, USA, Canada, Australia, Japan

Cover: Foto ©ninafisch / pixelio.de

More available books at **www.hansebooks.com**

GEORGIA

BEFORE THE

Senate Judiciary Committee,

WASHINGTON, D. C., FEBRUARY 9, 1870,

At a meeting of the Judiciary Committee of the United States Senate, the Chairman, Mr. Trumbull, said :

The papers before the Committee are the resolution of the Legislature of the State of Georgia, ratifying the proposed Fifteenth Amendment to the Constitution of the United States, February 7, 1870 ; the resolution ratifying the proposed Fourteenth Amendment to the Constitution of the United States, and the assent of Georgia to the conditions imposed by the act of June 25, 1868. These are the papers that were presented to the Senate the other morning, and have just been printed.

Mr. Caldwell and several other gentlemen called upon me day before yesterday, and stated that they desired to present to the Committee some matters in regard to the state of affairs in Georgia, and I informed them that the Committee would meet here at 11 o'clock to-day. I suggested to them that they should put in writing the points that they wished to submit to the Committee.

Before we proceed I would remind these gentlemen that we have but an hour—from now until 12 o'clock—and it is necessary that they should avoid extraneous matters, and be as brief as possible in presenting their points.

MR. BRYANT. Mr. Chairman, and gentlemen of the Committee :

We are here as Republicans who are opposed to the organization of the Legisture as it at present exists. This Committee requested Mr. Caldwell and myself to draw up and present a statement of our views. Mr. Caldwell will first open his

remarks and read a portion of the argument, and I will follow
with the remainder. The argument is in writing, and we will
be as brief as possible and not weary your patience.

MR. CALDWELL said: Mr. Chairman, and gentlemen of
the Judiciary Committee, we come here as Republicans from
Georgia, to relate the perils and sacrifices attending our efforts
to establish a republican party in the State, and appeal to you
as Georgians concerning the welfare of our State, and the future
peace and prosperity of our people.

I propose, therefore, in the name and in behalf of my associ-
ates, and those with whom I act. and whom, as a delegation,
we represent, to present a plain and unvarnished statement of
facts with the inferences that may be drawn from them, trusting
that you, in your wisdom, will devise a remedy for existing
evils, and to your sense of justice to redress the evils of which
we complain.

Georgia, as you are aware, proceeded to carry out in good
faith the reconstruction acts of the 39th Congress. A Convention framed a constitution, which was submitted to the people
for their ratification It was ratified by a large majority. The
great mass of voters, some 200,000, participated in the election.
It was as free and impartial an election as was ever held in
Georgia, the polls being named and the election being conducted
under the military supervision of Major General Meade, the
district commander. At the same time a governor, county officers, members of Congress, 44 state senators and 173 representatives were elected, two counties entitled to one member each
making no returns.

The Constitution being submitted to Congress, it was, in the
main, approved by that body, and an act was passed declaring
the State of Georgia entitled to representation in Congress
whenever the Legislature should comply with certain fundamental conditions. Upon the 25th day of June, 1868, General
Meade issued a proclamation convening the Legislature so elec
ted at Atlanta, on the 4th day of July. Only the names of
those who were declared elected by General Meade appeared in
that proclamation. These proceedings are printed in the Jour-

nal of the House of Representatives for 1868, which we present
for your inspection. The members were sworn in by Judge
Erskine, the person appointed by General Meade, and the Hon.
Rufus B. Bullock. Governor elect, who was acting at the time
as Provisional Governor, appeared and was sworn to support
the Constitution of the United States, and of the State of
Georgia. No other oath was required, and it was the oath
recommended and approved by General Grant.

From that time on each member was bound, in all the subsequent legislation in which he participated, by his oath, to support the Constitution of the State. And we are not aware that
Congress has passed any act since then relieving him from the
obligation of that oath. No question was raised there at the
time the members were qualified, and no objection made to the
eligibility of any of them on any ground whatever, but all who
were named in the proclamation of General Meade were allowed
to qualify. Each house proceeded to elect and qualify its
officers. The President of the Senate and all its other officers
were the regular nominees of the Republican party. The
House elected the Republican nominee for Speaker, and then
adjourned until Monday, July 6th. The parties then split on the
other officers, the Democrats electing a clerk and messenger, and
the Republicans a door-keeper. On a join thallot, as was afterwards ascertained, the Republicans had a clear majority of 13.
As soon as the two Houses were organized, Provisional Governor Bullock suggested to General Meade that there were persons
holding their seats in each House who were ineligible under the
14th Amendment, and the General ordered both Honses to suspend all other business and proceed to inquire into the eligibility
of its members. A resolution was adopted by each House,
after the investigation, declaring all of the members eligible to
their seats. This done, there was a clear Republican majority
in each branch of the Legislature, or else neither could have
elected its Republican nominees. The names of the members
were called *eo nomine* by the proper officers, and they
voted *viva voce*, as the Constitution requires. General Meade
approved of the course pursued by each House in the inves-

tigation determining the question of eligibility, and the Legislature immediately ratified the 14th Amendment, and adopted the fundamental conditions required by Congress. Hon. Rufus B. Bullock was then inaugurated as permanent Governor, and he swore to support the Constitution of the United States and the Constitution of the State of Georgia. His term of office, according to an ordinance of the Convention providing for the first election under the new Constitution, was to extend from the time of his inauguration until four years from the following January, or until January, 1873, when his successor, who should be elected in November should be qualified. One-half of the Senators were to hold until January, 1873, when their successors should be qualified, and the other half with all Representatives, until January, 1871. The theory of his Excellency now is that the late act of Congress to promote reconstruction in Georgia invalidates all the acts of the Legislature which preceded it, and that, consequently, his own term of office is extended until four years from next January. The term of one-half of the Senators is also extended until four years from that time, and the term of the other half of the Senators, and of all the Representatives, until January, 1871, thus giving to all an extension of two years beyond the time meant by the Constitution, or intended by their constituencies. Such is his pretension, sir, based on the plain and simple Act of Congress of December last But it would be well to see how inconsistent is this ·resumption with his former declarations and acts.

In his Inaugural Address he congratulated the coun'ry on the completion of reconstruction in Georgia, and the same day he gave a banquet at his own house over the restoration of the State to her proper relations with the Union. But, mark you, this was before the election of the United States Senators. In due time that election was held, and the result was different from what his excellency had anticipated Hon. Joshua Hill, a distinguished Union man and a Republican, was elected for the long term, and the Hon. H. V. M.

Miller, an old Whig, and a member of the Constitutional Convention, and an earnest friend of reconstruction, the chairman

of the committee appointed to revise the work of the eight
committees, to whom was assigned different parts of the constitution that was to go before the people for adoption, was
elected for the short term   This was done without concert or
agreement between them.   Mr. Hill, on the first ballot, received
only the votes of Union men and Republicans ; leaving off all
those who voted for Mr. Miller, who have since been declared
ineligible, he had a clear majority of 7.   By the same rule,
Hon. Joseph E Brown, the regular Republican nominee, had
a majority of 3.   Governor Bullock certified officially to the
election of Messrs. Hill and Miller, and in that certificate
declared that they were legally elected.

After the election of United States Senators, the Legislature
went into the election of State House Officers, and all the
Republican nominees were elected, still showing that the position of the Legislature was decidedly Republican.   Leaving out
all who since their election have been found or declared to be
ineligible, it will be seen by the estimates made by the Senators
that they were elected by a majority of the legal voters, those
who were the Governor's supporters, and who favored the election of State House Officers.   In various ways, and especially
in his published official acts, Governor Bullock did recognize or
assume that this was the first organization of the General
Assembly.   General Meade did the same ; Congress did
the same, at any rate the House of Representatives did, in the
very act by which certain Representatives from Georgia were
seated.

My statement thus far covers about two months of this
period.   From the first meeting of the General Assembly, on
the fourth day of July, 1868, and after the time that these elections were held, many acts were passed by the Legislature, some
of them involving great financial interests, and no one ever
suggested the idea, nor did any one dream that the idea would
be suggested, that the Legislature was illegally organized, or
that any act had been done that in the slightest degree vitiated
its proceedings.

Then, in the month of September, came the expulsion of the

colored members. That act I, and those associated with me, regarded as unconstitutional and unjust. We did not defend nor excuse it. But we respectfully ask you to consider the charges which have been made against that body by the Governor, and those who act in concert with him. He has evidently made that ground the salient point from which he has reached a result that he would gladly have had some excuse for without it. He has made it the occasion for asking Congress to pass a law giving into his hands more than extraordinary powers, powers which he has seen fit to assume, although the act passed by Congress does not grant them.

The colored members were expelled partly from Republican votes, and among them the Speaker of the House of Representatives, who was Governor Bullock's favorite candidate in the recent election for Speaker. Some Republicans voted against it and some voted for it, and others refused to vote at all, and some of those who voted for the expulsion of these colored members and some of those who refused to vote at all, are now with his Excellency asking that the former proceedings of the Legislature may be set aside as invalid. There are some who defended the colored members in the House, and voted against their expulsion, and with me they beseech you to see that the act of Congress is carried out strictly and in good faith, without any violation of its provisions. The Governor has made the expulsion of the colored members an occasion for the accomplishment of puposes that lie deeper than was anticipated by Congress when it passed the act in December last. It has long been manifest to some true Republicans in Georgia, that the restoration of the colored members to their seats in the Legislature was the ostensible object, not only for securing the reorganization of the Legislature, but the ripping up of every act preceding that reorganization; and he assumes that he has the authority, under the recent act, to accomplish that object; and he comes here to ask that you tolerate that assumption. He has proceeded without a single check in the exercise of his purposes, and wishes to still pursue his policy without restraint. This assumption is this, that the late act of Congress makes the whole State Government of the State of Georgia, under the act of December 22, null and void ; that there has been no meeting of the Legislature elected in April, 1868, except the one that was authorized by the late act; that there has been no legal election of United States Senators, or State House Officers, and that the official term of the members of the Legislature must be extended two years beyond what was intended at the time of the election. Such is his theory, and a glance at the formation of our State Government will most fully illustrate the practical effect of this theory.

There are three Judges of the Supreme Court, seventeen Judges of the Superior Court, and the same number of Solicitors General, all of whom are appointed by his Excellency. Besides these, there is a large number of notaries public, who are ex-officio justices of the peace, appointed by the Governor. All these must be removed and their places filled with reappointments. This is his theory—to overturn our entire judiciary as it has been organized But this is not the worst. We have eminent jurists in our State whose reputation is coextensive with our country. Some of these, and other high officials, have become personally objectionable to his Excellency, and he wishes you to let him displace them by the practical operation of his theory. He would have their places vacated under the operation of this act, that he may fill them with his new favorites. Sad as are these consequences of the Governor's assumption, there are others much more pernicious. A personal friend of the Governor's, a member of the Senate, who was present the first day of the session, on the 10th day of January, was explaining to me what the effect of the Governor's theory would be in regard to the point I have mentioned, and emphasizing the fact that it would involve an extension of official terms, and especially the membership of the Legislature ; he added, with an air of triumph, " you know that members will not vote themselves out of the Legislature when they have a chance to remain in for two years longer." I give the substance of the remark, but I have seen that that was the effect produced upon the minds of certain members, and we

know that Governor Bullock is too shrewd a politician not
to take advantage of such a fact   But what influence
must such a theory exert, and what must be the effect
upon the Republican party throughout the Nation.   If Congress should lend its sanction to such a theory, I trust
that in the wisdom of your Henorable Committee, measures
may be devised to avert the calamity that I fear would ensue
It is inconceivable that honorable Senators and Representatives could ever have meant tha ttheir laws should be carried out
in the way they have.   It is inconceivable that they should lend
the influence of their great name to do only certain things, and
at the same time have designed that the Governor should do
other things besides these expressly enjoined.   To require
nothing more of the Legislature than to reseat the colored
members, and, at the same time, to have another purpose in
view.   It is inconceivable that they should have had the double
purpose—a purpose that the Governor should use their laws
to overthrow the Government that had been previously established.   The Governor had no authority from the acts of Congress to appoint a clerk *pro tem.*, to organize the House, to call
himself a Provisional Governor, nor to treat the Legislature as a
provisional Legislature, nor to prevent any member from taking
one of the oaths prescribed by Congress, nor to call upon the
military to determine the eligibility of members, nor to put out
of the Legislature any one whom they might declare ineligible,
nor to put in their places those who have received the next
highest number of votes, nor to require the re-ratification of the
14th amendment, and yet, without having any of these powers
conferred upon him by the act, he has been guilty of a flagrant
violation of the law.

First. In calling upon the Attorney General to give a written
opinion as to the scope of the oath required by Congress.

Second, In endeavoring by the influence of that opinion which
was published in an Atlanta paper the day before the Legislature convened, to deter members from taking the oath who were
not disqualified by the 14th Amendment   This was done, and
by reason of it, many who in reality were not disqualified, did

not take the oath. The approval and endorsement of the opinion by General Terry, caused it to assume an importance which
would not otherwise have been attributed to it. This opinion
was promulgated, while the opinions of able lawyers upon the
subject have been withheld.

Third. By the appointment of A. L. Harris, one of his Excellency's employees upon the State Road as Clerk *pro tem.* to organize the House. Each member was sworn to support the
Constitution. The Code which was adopted by the Constitution,
provided how the House should be organized, and the officers
who should organize it. That Code, in sections 169 and 170,
says how the Houses shall be organized

Fourth. By appointing a Register in Bankruptcy to swear in
the members The Code requires that they shall be sworn in by
one of the Supreme Court Judges.

Fifth By an arbitrary order, directing the Clerk to entertain no motions of any kind, even motions pertaining to the
organization, and by the action of the Clerk in adjourning the
House from day to day without a motion from a member, in
order that the organization shall be, as far as possible, subservient to the schemes of his Excellency.

Sixth. By his asking for a military commission to inquire
into the eligibility of members

Seventh. By preventing members in both Houses from taking
the oath who would have been declared eligible. They
did not take the oath, induced by various threats and persuasions not to take it, but, by the ruling of the board of officers in
other cases, they would have been declared eligible. They were
prevented from taking the oath.

GOVERNOR BULLOCK. How prevented?

Mr. CALDWELL. In various ways. I cannot specify them
in detail now. I desire to finish my argument. I do not wish
to treat you with any discourtesy, Governor, but my time is
short, and you will have an opportunity of answering.

Ninth. By preventing the organization of the House by
causing members who were declared eligible to appear before a

board of officers not provided for by the law, to sit in judgment upon their eligibility.

Tenth. By causing some who had qualified to be prohibited from taking part in the organization of their respectize Houses

Eleventh By causing two persons, Mr. Wilcher and Mr Bennett, who were declared eligible, to be prevented from participating in the organization of the House.

Twelfth. By calling upon the military under the pretense of carrying out the provisions of the Act, no resistance being offered to the organization of either House under that Act ; but, on the contrary, all the members showed a willingness to organize in strict conformity to its provisions, and the only objection which was interposed was as to the illegal manner of the proceedings.

Thirteenth. By the manner in which he suffered, I do not say that he did it himself, but the way he suffered persons to be intimidated, and thus preventing them from qualifying, as is illustrated in the case of some of the members who became apprehensive of being harrassed by prosecutions if they should take the oath. Inducements were held out to some of them, which caused them unwarily to commit themselves to a position which implies their own ineligibility. They were advised to make application to Congress for relief from political disabilities. Promises were held out to them that Congress would relieve them, and they could then take their seats. And they were not aware of the fact that their applying to be relieved of their political disabilities disqualified them until General Terry assented to an order declaring that such applications were evidences of ineligibility.

Fourteenth. By allowing a Senator who had taken the oath, to withdraw the same from the office of the Secretary of State, when its removal would be evidence in an action for perjury.

Fifteenth. By admitting persons in both Houses to seats in both Houses who have not been elected by a popular majority, the only shadow of law for such a proceeding being found in section 121 of the Code, to which I refer your Honorable Committee To be brief, this section does not cover members of the Legislature, for the following reasons.

First. The officers referred to in this section are executive officers, entrusted with the execution of laws. They are not legislators charged with the making of laws. The Code is divided into parts, each part into titles, each title into chapters, chapters into articles, articles into sections, some of the sections have several subdivisions, as section 120, the one immediately preceding the one in question, and closely connected with it. This section is in Title III, which is headed "Executive Department." Title IV is the "Legislative Department," which shows no such provision.

Second. The officers alluded to are such as are elected by a plurality, but there is no law in Georgia which says that a plurality may elect a member of the Legislature. There are learned judges here with his Excellency to-day, and I challenge them to point out in our Code any such law of force in the State of Georgia to-day.

Third. The officers whose places may be filled by person having the next highest number of votes, must be found to be ineligible under one of the rules laid down in section 120—the section immediately preceding the one in question—and if found qualified, are declared to be eligible. The 14th Amendment is not enumerated among them. Our Code was adopted before that article came up.

Fourth. It is unconstitutional to apply this section to a member of the Legislature, for the Constitution gives each House the sole right to pass upon the qualification of its own members. Neither the Code, nor any legislative enactment can deprive members of that right.

Fifth. The officers referred to are such as are commissioned. Members of the Legislature are not commissioned.

Sixth. There is no precedent in the history of parliamentary proceedings for such action.

Ques. How was it that those who received the next highest number of votes obtained their seats in the last organization?

Mr. CALDWELL. The Legislature was addressed by a message from the Governor requiring it, and then they were seated by the majority, against all the remonstrance and argument that could be brought by the minutes as it was first organized

Mr. BRYANT. It was done by the previous question.

Mr. CALDWELL. Finally, Mr. Chairman and gentlemen of the Committee, I beseech you, in behalf of my fellow citizens, to save the people of Georgia from the consequences of so many flagrant violations of the law. I ask that the wrongs inflicted by the Governor may be redressed. I beseech you not to suffer the financial interests of a great people to be placed in the hands of one who has shown such a reckless disregard of law. I pray you to rescue our State from wrong and degredation that has scarcely any equal.

I thank you, gentlemen of the Committee, for your courtesy and indulgence in permitting me thus to express before you the sentiments of my people.

The CHAIRMAN. You can have your argument printed and presented to the Committee in that way.

Mr. CALDWELL. There is one correction that I would lik to make concerning a section of the Code.

The CHAIRMAN. You can correct it before it is printed.

Mr. BRYANT. Before beginning my argument, I wish to state in regard to this motion regarding the message of his Excellency the Governor, proposing to seat members in the place of those who had been declared ineligible.

We rose to a point of order that the motion could not be entertained. That point the Speaker decided against us. We appealed from his decision, and the appeal was sustained by a majority. The next morning another resolution was introduced by a member of the House, and the leader of the Governor's friends in the House made a short speech, in which he said: "You see that General Terry wants this done, and we tell you," (I give the substance of his words,) "that if you don't do it you will suffer from the military, and you have suffered from the military long enough."

In behalf of the State of Georgia. the Republican party, and the General Assembly of that State, I appear before you to-day to inform you that the Act of Congress, passed the 22d day of December, to promote reconstruction in the State of Georgia, has been violated in the organization of the Legislature, and ask that you prove to the people of the country and t . the people of Georgia, that you require Republicans as well as Democrats to obey your laws.

My friend, Mr. Caldwell, referred to the reasons which prompted you to pass the Act of December 22 The reconstruction acts were violated by the General Assembly of Georgia. Legally elected members of the Legislature were excluded from seats in that body, and men not entitled to their seats were admitted and allowed to participate in its proceedings Mr. Caldwell and myself were the only white members of the House of Representatives who made speeches against the expulsion of the colored members. We voted against their expulsion. We protested against the action of the House in expelling them, But we were opposed to the effort of Governor Bullock to require members of the General Assembly to take the test oath, or the iron-clad oath, as it was familiarly called. We opposed the bill introduced in the House by Mr. Butler, but we favored the bill introduced into the Senate by Senator Edmunds and Senator Carpenter. In other words, we desired that Congress should pass an act by which the colored members should be re-seated, and those who were ineligible under the 14th amendment should be excluded, but we were opposed to any further congressional action.

In conformity with the provisions of the law of Congress passed December last, to promote reconstruction in Georgia, Governor Bullock issued his proclamation, summoning all members elected under the proclamation of General Meade. to appear on the 10th day of January. at Atlanta. for the purpose of organizing in conformity with such act of Congress. Section 1st of this act the committee will remember.

The persons named in the above act had reference to the persons elected to the General Assembly of Georgia, as appears by the proclamation of General Meade, and the act declares that when they meet they shall proceed forthwith to perfect their organization. The exact language is, "And thereupon the said General Assembly shall proceed to perfect its organization, in conformity with the Constitution and Laws of the United States, and according to the provisions of this act." In violation of this act, Governor Bullock directed one A. L. Haris, Supervisor of the State Road, beloning to the State of Georgia, to act as Clerk, or Speaker *pro tem.*, during the organization of the House. Mr. Harris is an appointee of Governor Bullock, and can be removed by the Governor at pleasure. He was practically completely under the control of the Governor, and by the direction of the Governor, Mr Harris assumed the right to adjourn the House when he pleased. Members were not allowed to participate in the proceedings, except to take the oath required.

By direction of Mr Supervisor Harris an attempt was made, on the 10th day of January, the day the General Assembly convened, to read an opinion of the Attorney General of the State of Georgia, in regard to the ineligibility of members. The opinion had been prepared by direction of Governor Bullock, for the purpose of hindering persons duly elected from taking the oath. The Attorney General is not regarded by the legal minds of Georgia as a lawyer of great ability, and, as is well known in Georgia, he has been a strong partisan ' of the Governor. His opinion was endorsed by the General commanding the district of Georgia, General Terry, but the ablest lawyers in Georgia, among them Chief Justice Brown and Associate Justice Warner, held that the opinion was not good law The opinion was published in the Atlanta papers, and a copy of the paper containing the opinion was placed on the desk of th Clerk.

It was also published in the form of a circular, and a copy was enclosed in an envelope and placed on the desk of each member It was currently reported that the Governor would prosecute for perjury any person who took the oath prescribed by Congress who were, in the opinion of the Attorney General of

the State, ineligible, although they might be deemed eligible by
the ablest lawyers in the State. It was also announced that
able counsel had been retained to prosecute those men It was
understood that Governor Bullock had prepared a list of persons whom he had declared ineligible, and if any of those persons whose names were on the black list should take the oath,
they would be prosecuted A colored member was selected to
present protests against all persons taking the prescribed oath
whose names were on the list aforesaid, should any of them
attempt to do so. The members were required by Governor
Bullock to take the oath publicly, although many of them had
taken these oaths and filed them in the office of the Secretary
of State, as required by law. I have been unable to find in the
act of Congress any authority for this interference on the part
of the Governor. As the members whose names were on
the black list came up to the Clerk's desk to take the oath
prescribed by Congress, the colored member mentioned above
presented a protest, which was read. These protests were
printed, and had been carefully prepared beforehand. It is
fully believed that the object of reading the opinion of the
Attorney General, the reading of the protests, and the threat
of prosecution for perjury, were intended to hinder and interrupt members from taking the prescribed oaths I know that
many who could have conscientiously done so were deferred
from taking the oath from the fact that they were unable to
bear the expense of a trial for perjury, and the mental excite-
ment consequent to the trial. It is impossible for me to con-
vey any correct idea of the means resorted to by the Governor
and his friends to prevent the members of the General Assembly from taking the oaths prescribed. His proceeding in appointing an employee of his own to organize and preside over
the organization of the Legislature of Georgia, his attempt to
prevent men from committing perjury by the reading of the
opinion of the Attorney General, the reading of the protests,
and by other means, which it was necessary to see to understand. It is impossible for me to describe it. He appointed
Mr. Harris, a man known to be an officer under him upon the

State road at that moment. There was **Foster Blodgett, a** man under indictment for perjury in the United States Court for having falsely taken the iron-clad oath, and it was for that reason, I suppose, he determined his friends should not be similarly situated. I do not believe that the proceeding was according to the law passed by Congress. I objected to the course pursued. As a man, as a Union soldier, as a Republican, I felt that the Republican party and Congress were being used to further the interests of a body of men. I love the cause advocated by the Republican party as I do my life. I perilled my life on the battle-field. I love the party that adhered to the Government during the dark days of the rebellion almost as I do the flag of my country, and I could not see designing men use the party for the purpose, as I thought, of gratifying their ambition, and plundering my adopted State. As a northern man, as a Union soldier I was indignant when I saw my party disgraced in the eyes of Southern men, some of whom had fought in the Confederate army, and that the whole scheme was under the control of a man then under indictment for perjury, who had fought in the rebellion, and assisted in organizing a vigilance committee to murder Northern men. Mr Harris would not recognize my right to speak, although I was duly elected a member of the House ; and he had no legal right to be where he was. I disputed his right to dictate to me, a representative of the people, and he instructed an officer, whom he called the Seageant-at-arms, to arrest me. I refused to be arrested by them, and one of them drew a pistol and threatened to shoot me. There was a scene of confusion which it is useless for me to attempt to describe. It is said that I was excited ; I presume I was, if the indignation which I felt manifested itself upon my features A committee was appointed to wait upon General Terry. He pronounced their proceedings outrageous, and prevented the further reading of protests One of the men, I say, who took the part of presiding officer over the organization of the House, was an officer of the State Road, under Governor Bullock, a man not duly elected member of the House of Representatives ; and yet that **man was there acting** without any authority of law, and assuming to dictate to us; a man who had no right there whatever. Do you ask why we permitted these men to hold their positions there? I answer that General Terry gave Governor Bullock the support of the military, with which he was safe. Suppose that ex-President Johnson, a few months ago, when he opposed the policy of Congress, had been able to enforce his views by the power of the military, what would have been the result? General Terry put a stop to some of the illegal and arbitrary acts of Harris, but for many days he delayed the organization, and refused to allow the House to perfect its organization in conformity with the law provided by the acts of Congress. The organization of the House would have been perfected in two days but for the illegal interference of Governor Bullock. The law of Congress was openly and willfully violated.

Section fourth, you remember. If I understand that section, says all persons elected to the General Assembly, as appears by the proclamation of General Meade, who complied with the provisions of the act by taking the prescribed oaths, were entitled to participate in the reorganization of the General Assembly. It will be noticed that section first of said act provides that the persons, as appears by the proclamation of General Meade, shall organize in order that the prescribed oaths may be taken. Section four provides that the persons elected as aforesaid, who shall have complied with the provisions of the act by taking one of the oaths prescribed in said act, shall reorganize it. It appears clearly to my mind, that the only thing was to allow the persons named in the said proclamation of General Meade, to organize for the purpose of swearing in the members, and that those of the persons named in said proclamation, who took the prescribed oaths, should proceed to reorganize by the election of the proper officers. If that is not its meaning, then I do not understand its meaning. But this was prevented by Governor Bullock and Mr. Harris, and General Terry, who sustained them. I do not mean to say anything against General Terry. I consider him a high-toned gentleman. I do not believe that he was in this ring at all.

Governor Bullock and his allies usurped their authority. General Terry organized a military commission to inquire into the eligibility of the members of said General Assembly, who had, in conformity with law, taken the prescribed oath, and it was ordered that certain members should not participate in the proceedings of the Senate and House of Representatives.

Governor BULLOCK. I would beg leave to interrupt you a moment. I think, in making use of the term military commission, you do a very great injustice to General Terry. It is well-known by everybody that it was simply an advisory board of officers convened for the purpose of inquiring into the facts, and in nowise a military commission

Mr. BRYANT. The act provides that the members of the House and Senate, who shall have been duly elected from their several districts, shall, after taking the oaths prescribed, proceed to organize the General Assembly. Three members of the House and two members of the Senate, who had been duly qualified, were declared ineligible by this military commission, and were not allowed to participate in the organization of their respective houses.

I have examined the act of Congress in vain to find there authority for the military commander to organize a military commission for such a purpose. Before the General Assembly was organized persons were allowed to take their seats. Before it was reorganized some members were not allowed to take their seats, and some other persons were admitted upon the ground that they had the next highest number of votes. That was in violation of the law of Congress and of the law of Georgia, as Mr. Caldwell has already shown.

Thus has your authority been defied, thus has law been violated, and thus has the General Assembly been illegally organized. We appear before you to ask that you will vindicate your authority; that you will not allow any person willfully to violate your laws, no matter what may be his position.

General Terry is a man for whom I have high regard, I may almost say affection; but if he were my brother I would not approve of his acts if he violated one of your laws. I am unable to account for the course of General Terry. If he has violated the law, it has been because, in the name of loyalty and right, he has been induced to do what, in my own opinion, I could not have done under similar circumstances. A distinguished officer of the Republic, no man admires his course during the war more than myself; but I cannot believe that his course will be sustained, distinguished an officer as he is.

A committee of Republican citizens of Georgia, several of whom are members of the General Assembly of the State has come to Washington for the purpose of informing Congress that the act to promote reconstruction in the State of Georgia has been violated, and to ask that the General Assembly may be reorganized in accordance with the law.

Mr. Caldwell and myself appear before you to.day representing that committee. It has been said that we come to Washington a self-constituted committee; that we appear here on our own responsibility; that the people of Georgia, Democrats and Republicans, are tired of reconstruction, and want no further Congressional legislation. I pronounce this statement false, no matter from whom it may come. The great mass of our people have been shocked by the acts of Governor Bullock, and we must confess frankly that we have little hope that Congress will interfere and sustain the Republican party in Georgia, such men as Chief Justice Brown, a distinguished gentleman and able lawyer and jurist, and Joshua Hill, that great Union man There are two Republican organizations in Georgia. We represent one of these organizations, the National Union Republican Club of Georgia, which numbers among its members, many of the ablest Republicans of the State. We are Republigans, and not Democrats; and as Republicans, we are opposed to usurpation of Republican principles. I am chairman of the committee, and am one of the legal members of the General Assembly, and I come to you to-day and say that our General Assembly has been illegally organized, and that we desire it shall be reorganized according to law.

It is natural that you should ask why we oppose the policy of Governor Bullock. I answer, that the Republican party in

Georgia believes that there are two objects aimed at in this illegal proceeding on the part of the Governor: First, the election to the United States Senate of Foster Blodgett, a man that is now under indictment for perjury before the United States Court ; to ask you, gentlemen, to put the State in such a position that a man now under indictment for perjury shall be elected to the Senate of this country—a man about whom I have an affidavit in my possession, and I have the testimony of citizens of Augusta, about whose veracity there can be no question, showing that he assisted in organizing a vigilance committee for the purpose of murdering Union men Is this a man to be chosen to the United States Senate ? Yet this is one of the objects contemplated by Governor Bullock and his friends. Will you allow this to be, gentlemen?

I believe another object is, the paying for a building in Atlanta, known as the "Opera House," in such a way that the ring can make money. I make this statement not unadvisedly. We are prepared with the proofs, if you desire it. I believe that they wish to cover financial operations which they cannot explain. They wish to get rid of the State Treasurer by their sweeping reorganization of State House officers, so that they can put their hands in the treasury and carry out their financial operations and schemes On one side of the Republican party here, are Governor Bullock, Judges Parrott, Harrell, and Gibson, Mr. Conley, Mr. Tweedy, Foster Blodgett—Mr. Nunnally is a democrat. I hardly know where to place him yet. On the other side are Dr. Angier, Mr. Bowles, Mr. Osgood, Mr Williams, and myself. With the exception of Mr. Caldwell, who was a minister during the war, and did not participate, we were all Union men. Two of us were Union soldiers, and officers of a colored regiment. Dr. Angier had nothing whatever to do. with the rebellion. His office was the headquarters at Atlanta for Union men before the rebellion. He went north and remained during the rebellion. Mr. Williams and Mr. Osgood had nothing whatever to do with the rebellion.

Governor Bullock was on the other side ; was superintendent of the Southern Express Company, and aided the rebellion very much in that way. Mr. Blodgett was an officer in a rebel company. Mr. Tweedy was also an officer in a rebel company. Mr. Conley is a Union man, and, I believe, an upright man, and I am sorry that he is in bad company. Judge Parrott was also an officer in the rebel army during the war. Judge Gibson was a rampant rebel. He was colonel of a rebel regiment. He was elected as a rebel judge over a Union man, adopted by the "b'hoy," the regular rebels; was considered as being opposed to reconstruction, and did nothing for our cause, and was not a republican until he went to the Chicago Convention. Governor Bullock afterwards appointed him judge.

There has been much said in the papers about our committee being democrats. As for myself, I never voted anything but a republican ticket in my life. My first vote was cast for John C. Fremont, and I have voted the republican ticket ever since, and always expect to, and I stand here to-day as a republican and ask you to sustain us. Unless this is done, you never can have a Republican party in Georgia, and, as a member of that party, I beg you to consider the matter.

I thank you, gentlemen of the committee, for the kindness and courtesy with which you have listened to me.

Governor BULLOCK. I do not think that there has been anything said here to-day worthy of a reply. If the gentlemen would submit the proof of the charges and allegations made against me, then I may be ready to reply. The gentlemen have seen fit to make me a target for certain accusations and charges, and I desire that they will furnish the proof to sustain their charges.

Senator CONKLING. There was a hearing before this committee upon another occasion, when you were questioned as to whether the word "office," as used in section 121 of the Code, did or not legally apply to members of the legislature What was the ground that you then maintained on this point?

Governor BULLOCK. The same ground I maintain to-day; that the Code does not necessarily have anything whatever to do with it.

By Mr. CONKLING :

Q. I asked you what was the ground that you then maintained, as to whether a member of the legislature was included as an officer under the construction of this section ?

A. The ground I then maintained, was that it was not included.

Q. By reason of the Code ?

A. Probably.

Q. Do you mean to say, Governor, that you maintained the position here before this committee that section 121 of the Code authorized the seating of members of the legislature who had received a minority vote ?

A. I was not questioned upon that point, and did not express my opinion. I could make an argument now upon the question of the right of the next highest, if you desire.

Q. Was it not maintained by you here upon a former occasion, and by those with you, that under this section of the Code the turning out of the colored members, and the placing in their stead men who did not receive a majority of the votes, was a bold usurpation ?

A. I did ; because the expulsion of the colored members was of itself wrong.

Q. Was not the act of the legislature in substituting these members in the place of the colored men, denounced by you here in this room, and those with you, as a bold usurpation, not warranted by the law ?

A. Admiting that the expulsion of the colored members in the first instance was right, it was not—I never so considered it, and I certainly have never expressed such an opinion upon it. It was the opinion of many of the ablest legal minds in the State, that it was a legal procedure under the Code to admit in the place of members who were found to be constitutionally disqualified, those persons who received the next highest number of votes.

Q. Did not one of your friends who were with you here, in the presence of this committee, give a challenge to any one to find in the Code or anywhere else, any warrant or authority for seating in the place of members of the legislature who were found to be disqualified, those who received a minority vote ?

A. The question was broached by the Senator from Vermont, as to whether the members of the legislature were elected by a plurality vote. It was denied that there was any part of the Code which shewed that members of the legislature werf elected by a plurality.

Q.. Why didn't you state your views frankly to the committee at that time. If this thing was legal, right and fair, why didn't you say so at that time ? It might have saved some misunder. standing.

A. I did not so understand it. I did not hold that those persons who received the next highest number of votes could be seated in the place of those colored members held to be disqualified, under the Code at all.

Q. Then you don't claim that they should be seated under your Code?

A. No, sir; the late procedure by the legislature was not taken under the Code at all, but under the general law covering such cases. I will make the argument if it will not be detaining the committee too long.

The CHAIRMAN. The Governor means, I presume, that under a general parliamentary law, that the votes of those who cast for a disqualified candidate are not counted, and that person who received the next highest number of votes, if eligible, is entitled to take his seat.

Governor BULLOCK That is the general proposition. I do not wish to be understood as holding a different position now from that occupied by myself on any former occasion, because I never expressed my own opinion as to whether the terms of that section might be properly applied to members of the legislature or not A very large number, I believe a majority, of lawyers in the State of Georgia hold that it does.

Q. By Mr. Conkling:

I understood you, and I have no doubt I understood you correctly, that you and your friends maintained two positions upon that subject: 1st, the authority of the Code; and, 2nd, that the act of putting men into the legislature who had no majority at the polls, was a sheer usurpation? I have no doubt I understood you right. Did you maintain that ground?

A. I did, as broadly and firmly as I maintain it to-day. I do say that the seating of persons in the places of expelled colored members who were not ineligible was a usurpation.

Mr. CONLEY I would like to state to the committee in reference to this Code. There have been some doubts about that section of the Code in reference to members of the legislature, and as to seating the next highest. I got the opinion of the person who codified, Judge Irwin, who is one of the ablest jurists in the State He said the same question came up and was discussed by the committee appointed to codify the Code, and they determined that it applied to members of the legislature, and so intended it.

Governor BULLOCK. I can submit my reply to the arguments read by the gentlemen in writing, at such time as may be designated by the committee, but I desire to claim the privilege, if an answer is made, of again replying to any new points that may arise.

The CHAIRMAN. In regard to that, I would state to the gentlemen, that so far as the transactions of this committee are concerned, it is not our custom to listen to any argument whatever, but to confine those who wish to be heard to a plain statement of facts, and although there has been something like argument this morning, yet I would admonish the gentlemen upon both sides, that it is not our practice to listen to any arguments, and to ask that you simply make a plain statement of your facts, and be as brief as possible.

Mr. STEWART. I wish the gentlemen would make an index, giving the names of the voters, and the yeas and nays in the first organization of the legislature on the expulsion of the negroes and the election of senators, and also the names of the voters and the list of yeas and nays in each branch of the present legislature upon the ratification of the 14th and 15th amendments, and the fundamental conditions.

Governor BULLOCK. I would ask, as a matter of justice to myself, that where allegations are made as to my motives, that instead of simply allowing these allegations to go on record to be considered by the committee, the gentlemen making them be requested to present facts to sustain them.

The CHAIRMAN. It is to be expected, Governor Bullock, that the committee will be governed by a sense of propriety in regard to charges that are made.

Mr. EDMUNDS. We are too old to believe things until they are proven.

The CHAIRMAN. The committee will adjourn until Saturday, February 12, at 10 o'clock. It is understood that in the meantime the arguments upon both sides will be printed, and will be submitted at that time.

WILLARD'S HOTEL,

WASHINGTON, D. C., *Feb.* 10, 1870.

Mr. Chairman and Gentlemen of the Judiciary Committee:

The foregoing pages present the result of a verbatim phonographic report of the interview which was sought for by Messrs. Caldwell and Bryant, to which I was invited by the following note :

ROOMS OF THE COMMITTEE ON THE JUDICIARY OF THE UNITED STATES SENATE.

WASHINGTON, *Feb.* 7, 1870.

SIR: J. H. Caldwell, C. K. Osgood, and others have applied to lay before this committee certain facts in regard to the organization of the Legislature and the state of affairs in Georgia. The committee has appointed Wednesday next, at 11 o'clock a. m., to receive them, when you can also attend should you think proper, with such others as you may desire.

Yours, very respectfully,

LYMAN TRUMBULL,

Chairman of Committee.

GOV. RUFUS B. BULLOCK.

I have caused this report to be made and printed as the basis of my communication to the committee at this time, because I desire to notice only what was actually and publicly presented to the Committee.

These gentlemen are not here as representatives of any party or people, except it may be a faction of the Democratic party of our State, who desire to persist in their reactionary disposition and to continue their objection to, and contempt of the reconstruction measures of Congress.

Having been advised that it was the purpose of these gentlemen to visit the capital, and knowing their disposition and willingness not to hesitate at any measures which would seem to promote their peculiar views and purposes, I deemed it a duty which I owed to myself as an individual, and to my official position, and to the people who have honored me with their votes, to place myself in a position to act promptly for their vindication should it become necessary.

There is little to be said in reply to all that has been laid before the committee, except to enter a general denial of the allegations that are made, charging upon me various acts which I have never committed, and various motives and purposes by which I have never been moved. But I will take up the specific charges made by Mr. Caldwell, and which are introduced by him with a statement, referring to myself, "that he has been guilty of a flagrant violation of the law."

"First. In calling upon the Attorney General to give a written opinion as to the scope of the oath required by Congress."

Absurd.

"Second, In endeavoring by the influence of that opinion which was published in an Atlanta paper the day before the Legislature convened, to deter members from taking the oath who were not disqualified by the 14th Amendment. This was done, and by reason of it, many who in reality were not disqualified, did not take the oath. The approval and endorsement of the opinion by General Terry, caused it to assume an importance which would not otherwise have been attributed to it. This opinion was promulgated, while the opinions of able lawyers upon the subject have been withheld."

The opinion was carefully prepared by the Hon. Attorney

General, was submitted to the general commanding the district of Georgia, and by him pronounced as being, in his judgment "a correct exposition of the law." In this communication of the general commanding, dated January 8th, he is pleased to say further, " I may be permitted to add that I can hardly think it possible that any persons who are not qualified to sit in the Legislature, will be so unwise as to attempt to take the oath, for, aside from the consequences which would result to themselves, such a course of action could hardly fail to impede and delay that perfect restoration of the State to its normal relations to the General Government which all good citizens desire."

The publication of this opinion was made so that all persons might have the benefit of the fullest advice touching the proper legal construction of the laws of the United States, which were then about to be enforced. And it certainly cannot be claimed as improper or a flagrant violation of the law, to give the widest publicity to it under a proper legal construction, so that all persons may act knowingly and properly under it. The opinions of lawyers, either able or otherwise, upon this subject have never been withheld by me.

"Third. By the appointment of A. L. Harris, one of his Excellency's employees upon the State Road as Clerk *pro tem.* to organize the House. Each member was sworn to support the Constitution. The Code which was adopted by the Constitution, provided how the House should be organized, and the officers who should organize it. That Code, in sections 169 and 170, says how the Houses shall be organized "

Mr. A. L. Harris was appointed the Clerk *pro tem.* because of his peculiar fitness, from his public experience as a member of the Constitutional Convention, and the presiding officer of State conventions, and other parlimentary bodies, to perform the duties which were required. The appointment of some person became necessary, from the fact that until each member had taken the prescribed oaths, they could not, without violation of the act, proceed to reorganize by the election and qualification of the proper officers of each House, and because the general commanding the district of Georgia concurred in the opinion "that no member can take any part whatever in the organization, until he shall, after the convening of the Legislature have taken the prescribed oath before an officer authorized by the laws of the United States to administer oaths, and have filed it with the Secretary of State, and consequently there must be initiatory action on the part of some other authority, such as was taken when this same Legislature was first assembled "

The Code of Georgia has no application to the organization of the two Houses, as provided for by the act of December 22. But, admitting that the Code did apply, the officers prescribed in the Code were not available, the Secretary of the Senate being dead, and the Clerk of the House disqualified

" Fourth. By appointing a Register in Bankruptcy to swear in the members   The Code requires that they shall be sworn in by one of the Supreme Court Judges."

A register in bankruptcy was *not* appointed to swear in the members.   A commissioner of the United States Court was requested to be present and to administer the oaths upon the application of the members, which was done.

"Fifth By an arbitrary order, directing the Clerk to entertain no motions of any kind, even motions pertaining to the organization, and by the action of the Clerk in adjourning the House from day to day without a motion from a member, in order that the organization shall be, as far as possible, subservient to the schemes of his Excellency."

So soon as all the eligible members had taken the prescribed oaths, the members, being so qualified, did proceed to reorganize by the election of a Speaker, and the very moment the election of the Speaker was decided, the clerk *pro tem.* vacated his seat. Precisely the same mode of proceedure was had in the Senate, and I have yet to hear any complaint touching the manner of its organization.

" Sixth. By his asking for a military commission to inquire into the eligibility of members "

A *military commission* has never been asked for, nor has one ever been organized.

" Seventh. By preventing members in both Houses from taking the oath who would have been declared eligible. They did not take the oath, induced by various threats and persuasions not to take it, but, by the ruling of the board of officers in other cases, they would have been declared eligible. They were prevented from taking the oath."

I have not sought or attempted to prevent members in either House, who were eligible, from taking the oath, nor have I used threats or persuasions upon this or any other subject. Nor have I conversed with members upon the subject of their eligibility, except at their own solicitation, and in response to their own interrogatories.

" Ninth. By preventing the organization of the House by causing members who were declared eligible to appear before a board of officers not provided for by the law, to sit in judgment upon their eligibility."

Not true.

" Tenth. By causing some who had qualified to be prohibited from taking part in the organization of their respective Houses."

Not true as to any member who was eligible.

"Eleventh. By causing two persons, Mr. Wilcher and Mr
Bennett, who were declared eligible, to be prevented from participating in the organization of the House."

Not true.

"Twelfth. By calling upon the military under the pretense of
carrying out the provisions of the Act, no resistance being
offered to the organization of either House under that Act; but,
on the contrary, all the members showed a willingness to organize in strict conformity to its provisions, and the only objection
which was interposed was as to the illegal manner of the
proceedings."

Not true, either as to calling upon the military, or as to the
willingness of members to organize in strict conformity to the
law.

"Thirteenth. By the manner in which he suffered, I do not say
that he did it himself, but the way he suffered persons to be
intimidated, and thus preventing them from qualifying, as is
illustrated in the case of some of the members who became
apprehensive of being harrassed by prosecutions if they should
take the oath. Inducements were held out to some of them,
which caused them unwarily to commit themselves to a position
which implies their own ineligibility. They were advised to
make application to Congress for relief from political disabilities.
Promises were held out to them that Congress would relieve
them, and they could then take their seats. And they were
not aware of the fact that their applying to be relieved of their
political disabilities disqualified them until General Terry
assented to an order declaring that such applications were evidences of ineligibility."

Not true. I have not "suffered persons," etc., as stated.

"Fourteenth. By allowing a Senator who had taken the oath,
to withdraw the same from the office of the Secretary of State,
when its removal would be evidence in an action for perjury."

If my memory serves me aright, this senator was a judge of the Inferior Court before the war, and gave aid and comfort to the enemies of the United States. Under a misapprehension as to what constituted aid and comfort to the enemies of the United States, this senator, as I am informed, under advice and persuasion, took the oath of office. But, after consideration, he felt that he had done so under a misapprehension of the true intent and meaning of the act, and desired to withdraw from the false position in which he had placed himself. As far as it was in my power, I aided him in this laudable purpose by communicating to the Senate the following, under date of January 14th, 1870:

"ATLANTA. GA., January 14, 1870.

" Hon. J. J. Collier, of the county of Dooly, has made appli cation to withdraw his oath, taken on the 10th inst., from the Secretary of State's office, the oath having been taken by him under a misapprehension.

"As all good citizens unite with the authorities in the desire that, in the language of General Grant, ' when reconstruction is effected, no loophole is left open to give trouble and embarrassment hereafter,' and as the objection made by Congress to our former attempt at organizing the legislature is founded upon the fact that disqualified persons were allowed to participate in the proceedings, I have promptly granted the application of the Hon. Mr. Collier.

" The presentation of the name of Judge Collier to the board of officers will be withdrawn.

" Very respectfully.

"RUFUS B. BULLOCK,
" Provisional Governor.

" J. G. W. MILLS, Esq.,
" Secretary pro tem."

" Fifteenth. By admitting persons in both Houses to seats in both Houses who have not been elected by a popular majority, the only shadow of law for such a proceeding being found in section 121 of the Code, to which I refer your Honorable Committee "

Not true. Persons were legally elected by reason of the fact that the candidates opposing them in the election, and who received a larger number of votes, were disqualified.

These persons, some of whom were colored, having good reason to believe that the prejudice against their color would prevent members who were disposed to do them justice from voting in favor of awarding them their seats, made application to myself and the General commanding, to see to it that their rights were not denied them. Upon their application, a communication was sent by myself to the Speaker of the House after he had been elected by the qualified members making a reorganization, reciting the names of all who had made application, and upon this information being communicated to the House, that body, by a majority of the votes of its own members, promptly granted them their seats

I arrive at the conclusion that these persons were legally elected and entitled to their seats without any regard whatever to the Code of Georgia, and base it upon the well established rule of law, that it is the duty of the voter to cast his ballot for a candidate who is legally qualified to hold the office or position to which he desires to elect him, and that where the elector votes for a disqualified man, he knowing, or having had opportunity to know that the candidate for whom he votes is disqualified, his ballot is a nullity.

This responds to the First, Second, Third, Fourth, Fifth and Sixth branches of Mr. Caldwell's fifteenth citation of flagrant violations of the law.

Mr. Caldwell makes a statement in regard to the election of United States Senators by the former legislative organization, which only becomes material if it should be admitted that the legislative organization referred to ever legally ratified the Fourteenth amendment, and adopted the other conditions required by Congress, to entitle the State to representation. I am disposed to consider the election of Senators as being a part of the procedure necessary to restoration; but an examination in the light of the facts as to disqualified members who participated in the election renders it quite apparent that neither of these gentlemen were elected.

On page 104 of the Journal of the House of Representatives, called session of the General Assembly, July 4, 1868, herewith transmitted, we find that 110 votes were cast for Mr. Joshua Hill, 94 for Mr. Joseph E Brown, 1 for Mr. A. H. Stephens, and 1 for Mr. C. W. Styles, making a total of 206 Necessary to a choice, 104, upon which Mr Hill was declared to have been elected. An examination of the persons voting at this time, shows that two senators who were disqualified, Messrs. Anderson and Moore, voted for Mr. Hill; that one senator who was disqualified, Mr. Graham, voted for Mr. Styles; that 18 dis. qualified members, viz.: Messrs. Burtz, Crawford, Drake, Donaldson, Ellis, of Spalding county. George, Goff, Hudson, Johnson, of Wilcox county, Kellogg, Long, McCullough, Meadows, Nunn, Penland, Rouse, Taliaferro, and Williams, of Dooly county, voted for Mr. Hill; and that two disqualified members, Messers. Brassell and Surrency, voted for Mr. Brown, making 23 disqualified members who participated in the election.

Take this number, 23, from the 206 votes cast, and it will leave 183 qualified votes. Necessary to a choice, 92. Take the 20 disqualified votes cast for Mr. Hill from his total number of 110, and it leaves him with but 90 legal votes, being two less than is necessary to elect.

A similar examination may be made of the vote for Mr. Miller, on page 106. Some typographical error seems to have occurred in summing up the number of votes received by each of the candidates. An examination of the list of names discloses for Mr. Blodgett 73, for Mr. Miller, 117, for Mr. Seward, 12, and for Mr Akerman. 7, making a total of 209. Necessary to a choice, 105.

In this election, four senators who were disqualified voted for Mr. Miller, namely, Messers. Anderson, Graham, Moore, and Winn, and 21 members who were disqualified also voted for Mr. Miller, namely, Messrs. Brassell, Burtz, Crawford, Drake, Donaldson, Ellis, of Spalding, George, Goff, Hudson, Johnson, of Wilcox, Kellogg, Long, McCullough, Meadows, Nunn, Penland, Rouse, Smith, of Coffee, Surrency, Taliaferro, and Williams, of

Dooly, making a total of 25 disqualified members who partici‑
pated in the election.

Take this number. 25, from the 209 votes cast, and it will
give us 184 legal votes, of which 93 were necessary to a choice.
Take these 25 disqualified votes received by Mr. Miller from his
117, and it will leave him 92 legal votes, one less than is neces‑
sary to a choice.

There is very little, if anything, new in the remarks of Mr.
Bryant, certainly nothing demanding extended attention.

The bare assertions of improper conduct on my part cannot
be noticed further than to say that when any kind of proof is
offered in substantiation of such charges, I shall be prepared to
meet it.

I have already invited the General Assembly to appoint a
Joint Committee to investigate any charges that had been or
might be made against me. The State Senate adopted a reso‑
lution to appoint such a committee, but on a motion to suspend
the rules for this purpose, in the House, these people and the
party with which they affiliate voted in the negative, and the
motion was defeated.

The organization of the House was provided for, in pre‑
cisely the same manner as in the Senate, and we find the objec‑
tion to the organization of the House, coming exclusively from
defeated aspirants for official positions under that organization

In the Senate all the members seem to have promptly and
quietly acquiesced in the organization.

Mr. Bryant claims to represent a certain political club, the
officers and the rank and file of which are, as I am credibly in‑
formed, all here, and which does not exceed a dozen persons in
number. Certainly Mr. Bryant will not attempt to deny that
before leaving Augusta, on the 4th, he communicated to his
Democratic friends in Atlanta, asking for the assistance of Mr.
Dunlap Scott, of Floyd county, Mr. Senator Burns, Senator
Candler, and others, requesting that a delegation should be sent
to Washington, of the ablest men, from all parts of the State.

It is unnecessary to add that there has been no such response to his wishes.

Mr. Bryant also seems to object to the fact that I have appointed to office persons who have participated in the rebellion. It is true that I have made such appointments; but they have been of gentlemen who were marked in their respective communities for their high position, worth, intelligence and integrity. Men who, having surrendered in good faith at the close of the rebellion, united with the friends of Congress in promoting the reconstruction of civil government under Congressional enactments. Such men have been appointed, and, should it be in my power, they will be again.

If the men of worth and intelligence in the Southern States are to be perpetually excluded from official position because of their action during the rebellion, the State governments there established would be reduced to the unfortunate condition of being dependent upon persons without visible means of support, and of uncertain habitation, with little or no material interest in the country, to fill positions requiring a high order of intelligence, integrity, and security.

It is also alleged by each of these gentlemen, that the opinions entertained by myself of the legal relations existing between the State government and the reconstruction acts, involves an extension of the terms for which the members of the legislature were elected. I am rather astonished that the men who make a boast of being the only white men who objected to the expulsion of the negroes from the body, should be the first to claim that the terms for which these men were elected, should be curtailed by the revolutionary action of the disqualified rebels who expelled them.

My views upon this branch of the subject, as upon any other of a public character, have not been withheld, and as they were only recently presented to the Representatives in the General Assembly and to the country in a message, covering the whole subject as I understand it, the same is herein repeated and reaffirmed:

To the Senate and House of Representatives
of the Provisional Legislature:

A correspondence with the Major General Commanding this District is herewith transmitted, by which you will be informed that your organization is recognized from to-day as being one properly prepared to enter upon the action required by the several reconstruction acts of Congress.

ATLANTA, GA., February 1, 1870.

Brevet Major General A. H. Terry, Commanding District of Georgia:

GENERAL: I have the honor to report that a Joint Committee from the two Houses of the Provisional Legislature have informed me that the Senate and House have perfected an organization by the election of the proper officers, after excluding from the roll of members persons disqualified under the Acts of Congress from holding office. The two Houses stand in recess until Wednesday next, the 2d instant, at 12 m.

I am, General, very respectfully,

RUFUS B. BULLOCK,
Provisional Governor.

- -

HEADQUARTERS MILITARY DISTRICT OF GEORGIA,
ATLANTA, GA., February 2, 1870.

HON. R. B. BULLOCK.

Provisional Governor State of Georgia:

GOVERNOR: I have the honor to acknowledge receipt of your communication of yesterday informing me that a Joint Committee of the two Houses of the Legislature has informed you that the Senate and House of Representatives have each perfected an organization by the election of the proper officers. In reply to it I have the honor to say that I think that the Houses are now properly organized for the purpose of assenting to and complying with the conditions imposed by Congress for the restoration of the State to its original relations with the nation.

I have the honor to be, very respectfully,

Your obedient servant,
ALFRED H. TERRY,
Brevet Major General Commanding.

Headquarters Military District of Georgia,
Atlanta, Georgia, Feb. 2, 1870.

OFFICIAL:
J. H. TAYLOR,
Assistant Adjutant General.

That a proper understanding may be had of your present political
condition, and our status under the several acts of Congress, which
have, from time to time, been adopted for the purpose of securing the
establishment of State Governments, republican in form, in this and
other of the late rebel States, it is important to review those acts, and
to carefully consider what has been done by ourselves towards a compliance with their provisions.

Such a review will establish the fact that the present legislative
organization, if accepted and ratified by Congress, is the first and only
legal organization *de jure* of this Legislature, and of the State Government, established by the votes of the people under the reconstruction
acts; and that this organization is based *exclusively* upon the election
held under the order of the district commander on the 20th, 21st, 22d,
and 23d days of April, 1868.

By an act of Congress, which became a law March 2, 1867, it is provided that—

Whereas no legal State Governments or adequate protection for life
or property now exist in the rebel States of Virginia, North Carolina,
South Carolina, Georgia, Alabama, Mississippi, Louisiana, Florida,
Texas, and Arkansas; and

Whereas it is necessary that peace and good order should be enforced
in said States until loyal and republican State Governments can be
legally established; therefore,

Be it enacted, &c., That said rebel States shall be divided into mili-
tary districts, and made subject to the military authority of the United
States, as hereinafter mentioned; and for that purpose Virginia shall
constitute the First District; North Carolina and South Carolina the
Second District; Georgia, Alabama, and Florida the Third District;
Mississippi and Arkansas the Fourth District; and Louisiana and
Texas the Fifth District.

Sec. 2. That it shall be the duty of the President to assign to the
command of each of said districts an officer of the army not below the
rank of brigadier general, and to detail a sufficient military force to
enable such officer to perform his duties, and enforce his authority
within the district to which he is assigned.

Sec. 3. That it shall be the duty of each officer assigned as aforesaid
to protect all persons in their rights of person and property, to suppress insurrection, disorder, and violence, and to punish, or cause to be
punished, all disturbers of the public peace and criminals; and to this
end he may allow local civil tribunals to take jurisdiction of and try
offenders, or when, in his judgment, it may be necessary for the trial
of offenders, he shall have power to organize millitary commissions or
tribunals for that purpose; and all interference under color of State
authority with the exercise of military authority under this act shall be
null and void.

Sec. 4. That all persons put under military arrest by virtue of this
act shall be tried without unnecessary delay, and no cruel or unusual
punishment shall be inflicted, and no sentence of any military com-

mission or tribunal hereby authorized affecting the life or liberty of any person shall be executed until it is approved by the officer in command of the district; and the laws and regulations for the government of the army shall not be affected by this act, except in so far as they may conflict with its provisions.

Sec. 5. That when the people of any one of said rebel States shall have formed a constitution and government, in conformity with the Constitution of the United States in all respects, framed by a convention of delegates elected by the male citizens of said State, twenty-one years old and upward, of whatever race, color, or previous condition, who have been residents in said State for one year previous to the day of such election, except such as may be disfranchised for participation in the rebellion, or for felony at common law, and when such constitution shall provide that the elective franchise shall be enjoyed by all such persons as have the qualifications herein stated for electors of delegates, and when such constitution shall be ratified by a majority of the persons voting on the question of ratification, who are qualified as electors for delegates, and when such constitution shall have been submitted to Congress for approval, and Congress shall have approved the same, and when said State, by a vote of its Legislature, elected under said constitution, shall have adopted the amendment to the Constitution of the United States proposed by the Thirty-ninth Congress, and known as Article Fourteen, and when said article shall have become part of the Constitution of the United States, said State shall be declared entitled to representation in Congress, and Senators and Representatives shall be admitted therefrom on their taking the oath prescribed by law, and then and therefore the preceding sections of this act shall be inoperative in said State.

Provided, That no person excluded from the privilege of holding office by said proposed amendment to the Constitution of the United States, shall be eligible to election as member of the Convention to frame a Constitution for any of said Rebel States; nor shall any such person vote for members of such Convention.

Sec. 6. That until the people of the said Rebel States shall by law be admitted to representation to the Congress of the United States, the civil Governments that may exist therein shall be deemed provisional only, and shall be in all respects subject to the paramount authority of the United States any time to abolish, modify, control and supersede the same, and in all elections to any office under such Provisional Government, all persons shall be entitled to vote, and none others, who are entitled to vote under the provision of the fifth section of this act. And no person shall be eligible to any office under such Provisional Governments who would be disqualified from holding office under the provisions of the third article of said Constitutional Amendment.

Under this, and supplemental acts, an election was held on the 29th, 30th, and 31st of October, and the 1st and 2d of November, 1867, for delegates to assemble in convention and to form a Constitution. The delegates then elected assembled in convention at Atlanta on the 9th day of December, and after framing a Constitution and adopting certain ordinances, adjourned on the 11th of March, 1868.

An election for the ratification of the Constitution so framed, for members of a legislature, Governor, &c., was held on the 20th, 21st, 22d and 23d days of April, 1868, and resulted in the ratification of the Constitution by a large majority of the voters, and also in the election of members of the Legislature, Governor, &c.

The result of this election was proclaimed by the Commander of the District, in General Order No. 90, dated June 25, 1868, and in accordance with the following act of Congress :

AN ACT to admit the States of North Carolina, South Carolina, Louisiana, Georgia, Alabama and Florida, to representation in Congress :

Whereas the people of North Carolina, South Carolina, Louisiana, Georgia, Alabama and Florida, have, in pursuance of the provisions of an act entitled " An act for the more efficient government of the rebel States," passed March 2d, 1867, and the acts supplemental thereto, framed constitutions of a State government, which are republican, and have adopted said constitutions by large majorities of the votes cast at the elections held for the ratification or repealing of the same : Therefore,

Be it enacted, That each of the States of North Carolina, South Carolina, Louisiana, Georgia, Alabama and Florida, shall be entitled and admitted to representation in Congress as a State of the Union, when the Legislature of such State shall have duly ratified the amendment to the Constitution of the United States, proposed by the Thirty-ninth Congress, and known as Article 14, upon the following fundamental conditions :

SECTION 1st. That the Constitution of neither of said States shall ever be so amended or changed as to deprive any citizen, or class of citizens, of the United States of the right to vote in said State who are entitled to vote by the Constitution thereof herein recognized, except as a punishment of such crimes as are now felonies at common law, whereof they shall have been duly convicted under laws equally applicable to all the inhabitants of said States ; *Provided,* That any alteration of said Constitutions, prospective in its effect, may be made with regard to the time and place of residence of voters : and the State of Georgia shall only be entitled and admitted to representation upon this further fundamental condition : That the first and third sub-divisions of Section 17 of the 5th Article of the Constitution of said State, except the proviso to the first sub-division, shall be null and void, and that the General Assembly of said State, by solemn public act, shall declare the assent of the State to the foregoing fundamental condition.

SEC. 2. That, if the day fixed for the first meeting of the Legislature of either of said States by the Constitution or ordinance thereof shall have passed, or so nearly arrived, before the passage of this act, that there shall not be time for the Legislature to assemble at the period fixed, such Legislature shall convene at the end of twenty days from the time this act takes effect, unless the Governor elect shall sooner convene the same.

SEC. 3. That the First Section of this act shall take effect as to each

State, except Georgia, when such State shall, by its Legislature, duly ratify Article XIV of the amendment to the Constitution of the United States proposed by the Thirty-ninth Congress. and as to the State of Georgia when it shall, in addition, give the assent of said State to the fundamental condition hereinbefore imposed upon the same ; and thereupon the officers of each State duly elected and qualified under the Constitution thereof shall be inaugurated without delay ; but no person prohibited from holding office under the United States or under any State by Section 3 of the proposed amendment to the Constitution of the United States, known as Article XIV, shall be deemed eligible to any office in either of said States, unless relieved from disability as provided in said amendment ; and it is hereby made the duty of the President within ten days after receiving official information of the ratification of said amendment by the Legislature of either of said States, to issue a proclamation announcing that fact.

which became a law June 25th, 1868. The members of the Legislature so elected were by the proclamation of the Governor elect convened in Atlanta on the 4th day of July, 1868.

On the same date the Governor elect was appointed Provisional Governor by the Commander of the district, under General Order No. 91, dated June 28th. 1868.

This act of Congress authorizing the assembling of the Legislature, it will be observed, required that

"No person prohibited from holding office, under the United States, or under any State, by section 3 of the proposed amendment to the Constitution of the United States known as Article XIV, shall be deemed eligible to any office in either of said States, unless relieved from disability as provided in said amendment."

The Legislature thus convened having been organized under the orders of the Commanding General without inquiring into the eligibility of its members as required by this act of Congress, his attention was called to the fact that persons disqualified by that act were then sitting and acting as members ; whereupon the Commanding General directed the body to examine into the subject of the eligibility and proper qualification of its members; and upon a resolution being adopted in each House that ALL the then sitting members were eligible and qualified, the Commanding General authorized the body to proceed with the legislative action required by the several laws of Congress to which reference has been made.

This legislative action was taken on the 21st of July, 1868, in apparent good faith, and members of Congress who were elected, as provided by an ordinance of the Constitutional Convention, to the Forty-first

Congress, were admitted to the last session of the Fortieth Congress upon presentation of certificates from the District Commander that they had received the highest number of votes in their respective districts. This admission occurred in July, 1868, and Congress adjourned on the 25th of the same month.

The Legislature, on the 29th of July, 1868, proceeded to the election of United States Senators, when, by uniting the entire vote of the disqualified members and the members who were opposed to the Congressional policy of reconstruction, with a few who had assumed to favor it, Messrs. Hill and Miller were declared to have been elected Senators, the former for the term ending March 4th, 1873, the latter for the term ending March 4th, 1871. Although, as has since been disclosed, if the twenty-five or more disqualified men had been excluded, neither of these gentlemen could have been elected, Mr. Hill's majority on joint ballot having been but *seven* and Mr. Miller's but *fourteen.*

This action having been taken and the District Commander having issued his order relinquishing military control, it was assumed that the requirements of Congressional law had become inoperative, and that the national authority was no longer effective in Georgia.

On the 8th day of August, 1868, a resolution was offered in the House of Representatives of the General Assembly, "denying the eligibility of colored men to seats upon the floor of the House," who up to that time had been acting as members, and on the 3d day of September following, twenty-six colored members were expelled. On the 12th day of September, similar action was perfected in the Senate, and all the colored Senators were expelled. On the 6th day of October, 1868, this organization adjourned.

Congress reassembled on the 7th day of September, 1868, when the credentials of one of the Senators elect, Hon. Joshua Hill, were presented in the Senate, and, upon objection being made, his credentials were referred to the Judiciary Committee. This committee, having examined thoroughly into the organization, and the revolutionary action of the legislative body, which had assumed to elect these Senators, and after having had the case before it for deliberation for many weeks, made an elaborate report to the Senate against the admission of Mr. Hill, in which that committee say:

"Your committee are of opinion that the act of June 25, 1868, which required that the Constitutional Amendment should be duly ratified, must be held to mean that it must be ratified by a Legislature *which has in good faith substantially complied with the requirements of law providing for its organization.*"

Referring to the fact that *ordinarily* the election and qualification of members of the State Legislature is not a subject to be inquired into by the Senate, the committee in their report, marked very distinctly the difference between a State which has uninterruptedly maintained its proper relations to the Union, and one like ours, in which a government is being organized under and by virtue of the authority of the United States. The committee say :

The election and qualification of members of the Legislature, *where the existence of any Legislature authorized to act as such is not involved,* cannot be inquired into by the Senate in determining the right of a Senator to his seat, your committee hold that the question involved in this case is not whether persons not entitled to seats in the Legislature were received by that body and allowed to vote upon the election of a Senator, but whether the body assuming to be the Legislature *violated the conditions upon which it was allowed to organize, by permitting disloyal persons to participate in its proceedings.*

In repelling the proposition that the action of the Legislature touching the eligibility of its members, under the law and the Fourteenth Amendment, together with the subsequent action in the premises by the District Commander, finally disposed of the whole question and debarred Congress from taking any action—the committee say :

Whereupon the two Houses went through the form of an investigation But from the evidence before your committee, the investigation does not appear to have been conducted in good faith, or with any intention either of finding the facts or of excluding persons known to be disqualified. A committee was appointed in each House. In the Senate the majority of the committee found all the members qualified, but there was a minority report which gave an abstract of the evidence and found four Senators disqualified. The evidence consisted of the admissions of the Senators themselves, which, if true, *they should have been excluded.* Yet the Senate passed a resolution, under the operation of the previous question, admitting them all.

* * * * * * * * * * * *

For the purpose of this report, however, your committee did not deem it necessary to ascertain the number of disqualified persons admitted. But the fact that any were knowingly admitted was not only a violation of the Fourteenth Amendment, and a failure to comply with the requirements of Congress, but *manifests a disposition to disobey and defy the authority of the United States.* If one could be admitted, why not all ? And will it be contended that if the entire body had been composed of men who had usurped the functions of the Legislature against the express provisions of the reconstruction acts, they could have complied with the provisions of those acts so as to create any obligation on the part of Congress to receive their Senators and Representatives?

The action of Congress in this matter is fully quoted, because of its importance, as the foundation upon which the subsequent action rests.

If our legislative organization had been perfected as required by the laws, there would have been no power resting in Congress to interfere which would not apply equally to the adhering States—New York or Massachusetts—but when it was ascertained that we had *not* complied with the laws, and had *not* organized the Legislature by excluding men who were disqualified by the law, Congress could in nowise be bound by the action of such a body, and the right, we may say the *duty*, of Congress to adopt such measures as seemed to them proper to enforce their own laws, was not only indisputable, but freely admitted. As will be subsequently shown, Congress and the President concur in requiring us to commence again the work of reconstruction at the precise point where a failure in the execution of those laws becomes apparent, *viz:* THE FOURTH DAY OF JULY, 1868.

That both Houses of Congress moved in harmony upon this subject is established by the adoption of the following preamble and resolution in the House of Representatives of Congress after the report of the Judiciary Committee was made in the Senate:

Whereas it is reported that the Legislature of Georgia has expelled the colored members thereof, and admitted to their seats white men who received minorities of votes at the polls, and that members of said Legislature who had been elected thereto by the votes of colored men joined in such action, and that *twenty seven disqualified white men hold seats in said Legislature, in violation of the Fourteenth Amendment to the Constitution and of the reconstruction acts of Congress:* and Senators from Georgia *have not been admitted to the* Senate of the United States ;

Resolved. That the Committee on Reconstruction be ordered to inquire and report whether any, and if any, what further action ought to be taken *during the Fortieth Congress* respecting the representation of Georgia in this House.

[Adopted January 23—yeas, 127; nays, 33.]

While this action was being taken by Congress, indicating plainly the desire, the judgment, and the purpose of the Government, this illegal legislative organ'zation of ours, on the 13th of January, 1869, reassembled, and after being in session until the 18th day of March following, refused to heed the recommendations then repeated to perfect its organization in accordance with the laws of Congress, by the exclusion of the disqualified persons and the restoration of members expelled on account of their color.

All that has since been done could then have been avoided. We all knew what was required of us, and should have promptly complied.

Valuable lives would have been saved. The peace, good order, and good name of our State would have been maintained, and our material prosperity greatly enhanced, by following the dictates of wisdom and ceasing useless and fruitless opposition to the inevitable. But unfortunately other counsel was heeded, and the policy of reaction and resistance prevailed at that time.

Congress assembled again on the first Monday of December, 1869, and in accordance with the recommendation of the President proceeded promptly to prepare and adopt an act to promote the reconstruction of Georgia, and thus overcome the obstacles which had been placed in the way of restoration by the men who had embraced every previous opportunity to defeat that wise and just policy which is involved in the Congressional enactments for the establishment of civil governments in this and other Southern seceding States.

The act under which you are now assembled and organized was adopted in the United States Senate on the 17th of December, 1869, by a vote of 46 to 9, and in the House on the 21st of the same month by a vote of 121 to 51, and became law by the approval of the President on the following day, thus displaying the united determination of Congress and the President that the machinations of defeated rebels should not prevail by civil proceedings after their armed opposition had been so signally defeated.

In accordance with the letter and the spirit of the action of Congress, the President, on the 24th of December, 1869, assigned " an officer of the army, not below the rank of Brigadier General "—Brevet Major General Alfred H. Terry—to the command of Georgia as a *Military District.*

I have thus recapitulated the facts covering our political history from the time of the adoption of the act of March 2d, 1867—which declares

" That until the people of said Rebel States shall by law be admitted to representation to the Congress of the United States; the civil governments that may exist therein shall be deemed *provisional* only, and shall be in all respects subject to the paramount authority of the United States, any time to abolish, modify, control, and supersede the same," &c. —

up to the present hour, and it will not, I think, be seriously argued that the right reserved by Congress in that act has ever been withdrawn by the action of Congress or expired by reason of any legal act of our own.

But the argument made by General Terry in his report is so cogent and conclusive that I repeat it here. I quote from Major General Terry's report, dated "Atlanta, Ga., August 14th, 186). *   *

"While I have been in command of the Department, I have endeavored to take no action which could not be justified by the letter of the law, even if Georgia should be held to be restored to its original relations to the General Government. I have confined myself to giving support to the civil authorities, and moving detachments of troops into some of the disturbed counties where their presence would exert a good influence, and where they would be ready to act if properly called upon. I think that some good has in this way been accomplished, but the great evil has by no means been reached. As a *Department* Commander, I can do no more; for whatever may be the status of Georgia, and whatever may be the powers which an officer assigned to command the *Third District*, created by the Reconstruction Acts, would possess, it is only an officer, so assigned, who could exercise them; they are not vested in me by my assignment to the command of this *Department*.

"Where, therefore the civil authorities are in sympathy with, or are overawed by those who commit crime, it is manifest that I am powerless. In this connection, I respectfully call the special attention of the General Commanding the Army to the reports in regard to the attempt made in Warren county to secure the arrest and punishment of persons charged with crime, which are to-day forwarded. It appears to me that the national honor is pledged to the protection of the loyalist and the freedmen of the South. I am well aware that the protection of persons and property is not, ordinarily, one of the functions of the National Government, but when it is remembered that hostility to the supporters of the Government, is but a manifestation of hostility to the Government itself, and that the prevailing prejudice against the blacks results from their emancipation—the act of the Government—it would seem that such protection cannot be denied them, if it be within the power of the Government to give it. I know of no way in which such protection can be given in Georgia except by the exercise of the powers conferred on Military Commanders by the Reconstruction Acts. The question whether these powers can still be exercised in this State, is a grave one. I should hesitate to attempt the discussion of it, were I not convinced of the absolute necessity of such action. Being convinced of that necessity, I venture to present my views to the General Commanding

" By the act entitled 'An Act to provide for the more efficient government of the rebel States,' passed March 2, 1867, it is provided in the 1st section thereof, that the States of Virginia, North Carolina, South Carolina, Georgia, Mississippi, Alabama, Louisiana, Florida, Texas, and Arkansas, shall be divided into five Military Districts, and subjected to military authority; and in the 2d section, that to each of the said Districts shall be assigned as a Commander an officer of the army not below the rank of Brigadier General   The 3d and 4th sections of the act specify the powers and duties of District Commanders; making it their duty " to suppress insurrection, disorder, and violence, and to punish, or cause to be punished, all disturbers of the public peace,' etc.   The 5th section prescribes the manner in which, and the conditions upon which, the rebel States may be restored to their normal relations to the National Government, and fixes the contingencies upon the happening of which the preceding sections shall become inoperative in said States respectively; upon the happening of which, military control in said States shall cease.   This section is as follows, viz :

" 'SECTION 5. And be it further enacted, That when the people of any one of the said rebel States shall have formed a constitution of government in conformity with the Constitution of the United States in all respects, framed by a convention of delegates elevated by the male citizens of said State, twenty-one years old and upward, of whatever race, color or previous condition, who have been resident in said State for one year previous to the day of such election, except such as may be disfranchised for participation in the rebellion, or for felony at common law; and when such constitution shall provide that the elective franchise shall be enjoyed by all such persons as have the qualifications herein stated for electors of delegates ; and when such constitution shall be ratified by a majority of the persons voting on the question of ratification who are qualified as electors for delegates, and when such constitution shall have been submitted to Congress for examination and approval, and Congress shall have approved the same, and when said State, by a vote of its Legislature elected under said constitution, shall have adopted the amendment to the constitution of the United States proposed by the Thirty-ninth Congress and known as article fourteenth ; and when said article shall have become a part of the Constitution of the United States, said State shall be declared entitled to representation in Congress, and senators and representatives shall be admitted therefrom on their taking the oath prescribed by law; and then and thereafter the preceding sections of this act shall be inoperative in said State : Provided, that no person excluded from the privilege of holding office by said proposed amendment to the Constitution of the United States shall be eligible to election as a member of the convention to frame a constitution for any of said rebel States, nor shall any such person vote for members of such convention."

It will be observed that, after prescribing the terms of restoration, it provides that, when they shall have been complied with by any one of the States to which the act applies, said State shall be declared to be entitled to representation in Congress : and *Senators and Representatives shall be admitted therefrom on their taking the oath prescribed by law ;* and THEN AND THEREAFTER the preceding sections shall be inoperative in said State.   I respectfully submit that, by this language, the actual admission of Senators and Representatives is made a condi-

49

tion precedent to the abrogation of military authority ; that the action
of the two Houses of Congress in admitting members was provided for
as the final recognition of the restoration of the States : and that, until
that recognition by the law-making power, unless subsequent acts have
changed, modified or repealed this act, in this respect, the powers conferred on District Commanders may be exercised.

The supplementary acts of March 23, and July 19th, 1867, to my ap-
prehension, have no bearing whatever upon this question ; they in no
degree modify or change the act of March 2d, in respect to the time
when, or the conditions upon which the first four sections of that act
become inoperative.

The act of June 25, 1858, the only remaining act which relates to the
government and restoration of the rebel States, seems to have been
passed mainly in pursuance of those portions of the fifth section of the
act of March 2, 1867, which provide for the submission to, and approval by Congress of the constitutions framed for the several States, and
for a declaration by Congress that the States are entitled to representation. It contains a conditional approval of the constitutions formed
for certain of the rebel States, and the reaffirming one of the original
conditions of restoration, provides that after the ratification of the
Fourteenth Amendment by the Legislatures of the said States, they
shall be entitled and admitted to representation. In this there seems
to be no departure from the original act ; that act also provided that
when the prescribed terms and conditions should be complied with,
the States should be entitled and admitted to representation, but it
made the cessation of military control dependent on the actual admission of Senators and Representatives ; and the act of June 25th leaves
this matter where the original act placed it. The plan of reconstruction contemplates five great steps. 1st. The formation of a State con-
titution. 2d. The approval of that constitution by congress. 3d. The
ratification of the Fourteenth Amendment. 4th. The declaration of
Congress that the State is entitled to representation ; and 5th. The
final act of recognition—the admission of Senators and Representatives on their taking the oath prescribed by the law. When all these
steps are taken, the powers conferred on military commanders cease to
exist ; until then they may be exercised. The persons elected as Senators by the Legislature of Georgia have never been admitted to the
Senate, and no Representatives from the State have been admitted to
the present House of Representatives. I therefore respectfully submit
that the work of reconstruction here has not been completed, and that
consequently the powers conferred on military commanders may still
be exercised within the State.

Thus far I have proceeded on the assumption that all the conditions
precedent to restoration have been complied with by Georgia, but I
now submit that the Fourteenth Amendment has not been duly ratified by its Legislature. The act of June 25, 1868, in its concluding
section, provides that " no person prohibited from holding office under
the United States or under any State by Section 3 of the proposed
amendment to the Constitution of the United States known as Article
XIV. shall be eligible to any office in either of said States, unless relieved from disability as provided in said amendment ;" thus in effect
prescribing the character of the Legislature by which said amendment
should be adopted as a condition precedent to restoration; that is to
say, Legislatures composed of persons eligible to office under that

amendment. *No such Legislature has yet assembled in Georgia;* for it is well ascertained that in the Legislature which did assemble and which acted upon the Fourteenth Amendment were a number of persons who were not eligible to seats therein. The facts in the case are fully set forth in the following extract from the report made in July last by a majority of the Judiciary Committee of the Senate of the United States, to whom had been referred the credentials of Mr. Joshua Hill, claiming to be a Senator elect from this State, viz:

"The District Commander, General Meade, by a General Order dated June 25, 1868, declared the result of the election, Rufus B. Bullock being elected Governor, and among the members elected to the Legislature in that order were thirty-one colored men—three Senators and twenty-eight Representatives. (See exhibit No. 1.) By a proclamation of the Governor elect, in pursuance of the act of June 25, 1868, the Legislature of Georgia convened on the 4th of July following. On the 8th July the organization of the two houses was effected, and all persons declared elected were allowed to take their seats.

"When the Governor elect was notified of the action of the two houses, he addressed a communication to General Meade, Commander of the District, informing him of the fact, and also that it was alleged that a number of the members of the General Assembly who had taken their seats and one or more officers of that body were not eligible under the act of June 25, 1868, by reason of their having taken an official oath to support the Constitution of the United States and subsequently had given aid and comfort to the enemies thereof. General Meade on the same day replied to the communication, and, among other things, desired the Governor elect to communicate to the Legislature that he could not recognize any act of that body as valid or allow the same to be executed until satisfactory evidence was produced that all persons excluded by the Fourteenth Amendment were deprived of their seats in both houses. Whereupon, the two houses went through the form of an investigation. But from the evidence before your committee, the investigation does not appear to have been conducted in good faith, or with any intention either of finding the facts or of excluding persons known to have been disqualified. A committee was appointed in each house. In the Senate the majority of the committee found all the members qualified; but there was a minority report which gave an abstract of the evidence and found four Senators disqualified. The evidence consisted of the admission of the Senators themselves; which, if true, they should have been excluded. Yet the Senate passed a resolution, under the operation of the previous question, admitting them all. These facts appear in the official correspondence between Governor Bullock and General Meade in regard to the organization of the Georgia Legislature. (See Exhibit A.) There were three reports in the House. The majority report found two members disqualified; one of the minority reports found still another member disqualified, but the other minority report found that all were qualified. The last report was adopted by the House under the operation of the previous question. To illustrate the manner in which the investigation was conducted, a copy of the proceedings of the Legislature on the 16th, 17th and 18th days of July, 1868, as reported in the Atlanta Daily Era, and forwarded to the State Department, is attached to this report. (See Exhibit A, B and C.) It is alleged that an impartial investigation would have shown from thirty to forty members of the Legislature disqualified under the Fourteenth Amendment, and although your committee have not been able to fully investigate this matter, but from the evidence before them, they have little doubt that the number was large, as the exhibit hereto attached will tend to establish."

It may be contended that this action of the two branches of the Legislature is final and conclusive; but I respectfully submit that by the terms of the act of March 2, the State government at the time was provisional only; the Fourteenth Amendment had not been ratified, the conditions precedent to restoration had not been performed, the State and its officers were still "subject to the paramount authority of Congress," and to the authority which had been conferred by law on the military Commander of the District, of which Georgia formed a part: therefore it was within the power of that Commander to determine the eligibility of members; and consequently the clause of the Constitution of the State which gives conclusive jurisdiction of this question to the two branches of the Legislature, cannot be considered as having taken effect.

And I also submit that the action of the Legislature admitting to membership the ineligible persons elected to it, whether intentionally so or not, was, in effect, a fraud upon the reconstruction laws, and upon the government; a fraud which so vitiates its organization that it cannot be considered a Legislature within the terms and provisions of the reconstruction acts: and therefore the Fourteenth Amendment has not been ratified by the Legislature of Georgia: the conditions precedent to the restoration of the State have not been fully complied with, and the first, second, third, and fourth sections of the act of March 2 have not become inoperative in this State.

There have been several official acts of the Executive and Legislative Departments of the Government bearing upon this question, some of which declare or imply that the State has been restored to its normal condition, others that it has not been. Of the former class are: First. The order of General Meade declaring the State restored, and withdrawing from the exercise of military control over it. Secondly. General Orders No. 55, Adjutant General's Office, Washington, July 28, 1868, declaring that the Third Military District had ceased to exist; and Thirdly. The admission of members from Georgia to the House of Representatives of the Fortieth Congress. Of the latter class are: The refusal of the Senate to admit the persons elected to it from Georgia; the refusal of the present House of Representatives to admit members to it from the State, and the refusal of Congress to admit members to it from the State, and the refusal of Congress to count in the accustomed manner the electoral vote of the State at the recent Presidential election. It is hardly necessary to suggest that the argument to be drawn from this action, as a whole, is strongly against the proposition that the State has been restored.

In conclusion, I desire to express my conviction that the only way to restore good order in the State, is to resume military control over it for the time being, *and ultimately to provide by law that the Legislature shall reassemble as a provisional Legislature,* from which all ineligible persons shall be excluded, and for which all eligible persons elected to it, white or black, shall be admitted. Such a Legislature would, I believe, enact such laws and invest the Executive with such powers as would enable him to keep the peace, protect life and property, and punish crime.

The process of resuming military control would, it appears to me, be a very simple one. All that would be required is an order from the President countermanding General Orders No. 55, Adjutant General's Office, July 28, 1868, and General Orders No. 103, Headquarters Third Military District, July 22, 1858, and assigning an officer to the command of the District, excepting the States of Florida and Alabama. This action I respectfully recommend.

I have the honor to be, General, very respectfully, your obedient servant,

ALFRED H. TERRY,
Brevet Major General Commanding.

That the foregoing presents the correct legal view of the case, and that Congress and the administration have so decided, is fully established by the fact that Congress has assumed to legislate upon the subject, and that the President has approved such legislation, and has assigned a commander to this district, by the following order :

GENERAL ORDERS } HEADQUARTERS OF THE ARMY,
{ ADJUTANT'S GENERAL'S OFFICE,
No. 1. } Washington, January 4, 1870.

By direction of the President of the United States, so much of General Orders No. 103, dated Headquarters Third Military District, (Department of Georgia, Florida and Alabama,) Atlanta, Georgia, July 22, 1868; and so much of General Orders No. 55, dated Headquarters of the Army, Adjutant General's Office, Washington, July 28, 1868, as refers to the State of Georgia is hereby countermanded. Brevet Major General Terry will, until further orders, exercise within that State the powers of the Commander of a Military District, as provided by the act of March 2, 1867, and the acts supplementary thereto, under his assignment by General Orders No. 83, dated Headquarters of the Army, Adjutant General's Office, Washington, December 24, 1869.

By command of General Sherman.

E. D. TOWNSEND,
Adjutant General.

That it is a political question upon which Congress is the sole and final judge, will not be denied.

It therefore follows that, having perfected an organization as required by law, you are prepared and required to pass upon the several subjects submitted for your action by the acts of Congress, known as the Reconstruction Acts, and to elect Senators.

These subjects are the ratification of the Fourteenth Amendment, giving the assent of the State to certain modifications of the Constitution, and the adoption of the Fifteenth Amendment.

Should it be urged that we have already acted upon the Fourteenth Amendment. etc., it is a sufficient answer to quote the action of Congress, wherein they hold that no legal organization of a Legislature has heretofore been perfected. And should it be argued that Georgia was counted as having ratified the Fourteenth Amendment, it is answered by the following joint resolution of Congress, adopted before Georgia acted, and in which Georgia is not named:

Concurrent Resolutions of Congress respecting the ratification of the Fourteenth Amendment to the Constitution, July 21 1868.

Whereas the Legislatures of the States of Connecticut, Tennessee, New Jersey, Oregon, Vermont, West Virginia, Kansas, Missouri, Indiana, Ohio, Illinois, Minnesota, New York, Wisconsin, Pennsylvania, Rhode Island, Michigan, Nevada, New Hampshire, Massachusetts, Nebraska, Maine, Iowa, Arkansas, Florida, North Carolina, Alabama, South Carolina, and Louisiana, being three-fourths and more of the several States of the Union, have ratified the fourteenth article of amendment to the Constitution of the United States, duly proposed by two-thirds of each House of the Thirty ninth Congress, therefore,

" *Resolved, by the Senate,* [the House of Representatives concurring,] That said fourteenth article is hereby declared to be a part of the Constitution of the United States, and it shall be duly promulgated as such by the Secretary of State.

" July 21—Passed the Senate without a count.

" Same day the House passed the resolution—yeas 126, nays 32 ; the preamble—yeas 127, nays 35."

Our action having been accepted and approved by Congress by the admission of Senators and Representatives, we will, after nearly ten years of wandering astray, be once more a State in the Union. Our Constitution will then become of force, and upon the election by your now legal organization of the officers provided for by the Constitution, the State Government will become a government *de jure;* the members of your honorable body will enter upon the terms for which they were elected, and it is hoped and believed that nothing will ever again occur to disturb the harmonious relations which should be forever maintained between this State and the National Government.

I transmit herewith authentic copies of the joint resolutions of the Thirty-ninth Congress, proposing an amendment to the Constitution of the United States, known as Article XIV, and the joint resolution of the Fortieth Congress, proposing an amendment known as Article XV; also the act of June 25th, 1868, which requires the assent of the State to be given to certain modifications of the Constitution of the State.

The party in this State which has promoted reconstruction may properly be mentioned in a communication of this character, because party lines here, as in all the Southern States since the rebellion, have been drawn between those who favored restoration of State governments under Congressional enactment and those who opposed such restoration ; the former party being in favor of compliance, and the latter party opposed to any settlement which did not practically yield all the issues which the General Government had established by force of arms.

This party, therefore, has been and is the party of peace, and the other the organization of all the elements of discord, discontent, and defiance. And I speak of the party favoring the reconstruction measures, now to recognize the fact that its course has been consistent and persistent in support of the measures provided by Congress as a settlement and for a restoration of civil government in the South, and the party has been equally as determined in its opposition to every scheme which the old political tricksters have devised to defeat this wise and just policy of Congress.

In pursuing their opposition to Congress, these political charlatans have resorted to every conceivable baseness, abandoning argument to take up with murder and assassination; disregarding principles to indulge in villification, and now, in their hopeless despair, we find them endeavoring to grasp a Republican livery, under which they hope to hide their nefarious purpose. They now loudly proclaim their hot haste to promote reconstruction and to adopt measures which will successfully perfect it.

While we congratulate the State, and the country, even upon this outward evidence that wisdom is returning to our misguided brethren, the party door is wide and open for any and all who desire to enter and support the great principles of equal rights and republican liberty, which have triumphed over secession and rebellion.

We desire the good of the whole people; that the rights of the poor laboring men shall be equally protected with those of the rich; that the avenues of intelligence shall be open for all, and that a citizen's worth shall be determined by his own efforts and his own character, neither advanced nor retarded by his birth, his color, his religion, or his politics. Upon this platform all can unite. The industrious, the intelligent, and those who love peace rather than strife, will soon abandon the lead of disappointed politicians, and aid in sustaining the Government.

The wrongs which have been done, the lawless outrages which have been committed in many parts of the State, are the acts of but a

few irresponsible persons. When all good citizens exert their influence in favor of justice, lawlessness will cease.

Let us, therefore, unite in a complete recognition of rights of *men*,
irrespective of birth, color, or previous condition, and frankly admit
that under, and before, the law all men are equal—that all are responsi-
ble—and see to it that by future legislation the requirements of our
Constitution are recognized—that free schools are established and
maintained, and that protection is secured for person and property,
and for the free expression of political opinions.

Let party lines be extended so as to welcome and include all who
are in favor of impartial suffrage and universal amnesty. Under our
state Constitution no man is disfranchised, and under the Constitution of the United States no man will be disqualified from holding
office who is ready to maintain and uphold the Government.

I would respectfully recommend that the Fourteenth Amendment
and the fundamental conditions required by the Act of June 25, 1868,
and the Fifteenth Amendment be adopted at once, and that your honorable body then take a recess until Monday the 14th instant.

Should it be deemed desirable by any member to attempt general
legislation at this time, his attention is invited to the following extract
from the opinion of the Honorable Attorney General of the United
States in the case of Virginia :

"It is required under the previous law to act upon the question of
adopting the * * [Amendments] to the Constitution of the United
States before the admission of the States to representation in Congress.
I am of opinion, therefore, that it may come together, organize, and
act upon that Amendment, but that until Congress shall have approved the Constitution, and the action under it, and shall have restored
the State to its proper place in the Union, by recognizing its form of
Government as republican, and admitting it to representation, the
Legislature is not entitled, and could not, without violation of law,
be allowed to transact any business, pass any act or resolve, or under-
take to assume any other function of a Legislature, if the test oath
has not been required of its members."

In a subsequent opinion the Honorable Attorney General decided
that the election of Senators, at the proper time, was a part of the
work of reconstruction.

Your organization having been recognized from to-day, the time
fixed by the United States for the election of Senators will occur on
Tuesday, the 15th instant, and as it is unwise to attempt any general
legislation while the government is provisional, and pending our
recognition by Congress, the recess recommended seems desirable.

I shall esteem it a personal and official favor if your honorable body will authorize a joint committee to sit during the recess, and investiga e the indirect charges made by the Treasurer, through the public prints, against the Executive, as well as any and all charges he may now have to present I would respectfully recommend that the Committee be authorized to send for persons and papers, and to administer oaths; and I am confident that such validity will be given to the acts of the committee, by the Commander of the District, as may be necessary to insure justice.

RUFUS B. BULLOCK,
Provisional Governor.

Atlanta, Wednesday, February 2, 1870.

The great mass of the people of our State desire a prompt settlement of the reconstruction measures, and are disposed to acquiesce in the congressional plan as now carried out, by means of the late supplemental act to promote reconstruction in Georgia.

I am confidant that the organization of the legislature is now as nearly perfect as it is possible by legislation to make it. That there are but few, if any, members of the General Assembly now participating in its proceedings who are disqualified, certainly not enough of that number to affect the action of either House. And I therefore respectfully recommend that Congress, being the sole and final judge of the question, shall accept and approve of the organization which has been made, and thereby close up and definitely settle the great cause of the restoration of the States to the Union with loyal local governments

RUFUS B. BULLOCK.

P. S.—As requested by Senator Stewart, I transmit herewith the list of yeas and nays in the House and Senate on the passage of the 14th and 15th amendments and fundamental conditions, as taken on the 2d of February instant.

I also transmit the following letter:

"NATIONAL HOTEL, WASHINGTON, D. C.,
"*February* 9, 1870.

"*Governor Rufus B. Bullock:*

"DEAR SIR: I was very much astonished this morning to hear Rev. Dr. J. H. Caldwell, of our State, objecting to the organization of our legislature, from the fact that only a few days before I left Georgia, Hon. J. Mason Rice, a member of the legislature, called on me and stated that Mr. Caldwell desired him to say to me, that if the party would elect him (Caldwell) senator for the long term, that he would sustain you as Governor, and work to unite the republicans on the same line.

"Hon. C. H. Prince also heard Mr. Rice say the same thing.
"Yours truly,
"FOSTER BLODGETT."

"The above statement was made to me by Mr. Rice.
"C. H. PRINCE."

www.ingramcontent.com/pod-product-compliance
Lightning Source LLC
Chambersburg PA
CBHW022034080426
42733CB00007B/825